Disclaimer

Joshua Therrien is not a financial advisor. This book is how I was able to create and multiply my personal income for a time in my life. Your results solely depend on what you put into your life and the decisions you make. The author is not liable for misuse, misconception and misinterpretation of information contained in this book. The author shall have neither liability nor responsibility to any person or entity with respect to any loss, damage, or injury caused caused directly or indirectly by the information contained in this book.

I0391040

Edited by William Gowen
Cover designed by Emily Therrien

Table of Contents

Endorsements

In his groundbreaking new book, Josh makes it clear how to stop earning a paycheck and how to truly create wealth. If you hate the idea of creating income streams that will build your wealth and freedom, DON'T read this book.

- **Joe Giglietti Amazon #1 Best Selling Author**

"Joshua Therrien is the real deal and so is the advice in this book. The nuggets of wisdom that lie within are both practical and challenging!"

- **Richard Trevino, Speaker Consultant and Author**

"When I think of Joshua, I think of the courage he has had to make the choices he has made in life when the odd's were against him. He is a man many should take seriously and grow from because he knows what he is talking about, everyone should buy this book and then some for their friends and family!"

- **Shane the Train, founder of www.shanethetrain.com**

"I have seen Joshua come from a McDonalds employee to an owner of multiple business' and an amazing non-profit Make-A-Change Inc. I am proud to say Josh truly knows what he is talking about when it comes to money, everyone should take a few moments and read this book!"

- **Mike Campbell, president of Platinum Productions, Incorporated**

I would like to thank my beautiful wife Emily for always being by my side and supporting me through all the crazy decisions we have made in life. I wouldn't be the man I am today without her and we wouldn't be doing so much if not for the support from my amazing wife. Emily, thank you for being my best friend, forever!

A Season for This and That

This book is not a get-rich-quick scheme. It's not a financial advice book. If that is what you are looking for, *stop reading*. I am about to take you on a trip into the choices that have made me get where I am and put me on the road of where I am going. The choices are based on pure logic. Because of what I am going to write about in this book, I am on my way to becoming an entrepreneur powerhouse. The goal of this book is to give guidance and motivation to get you on a better path toward a better freedom. Everyone's goals may be different. Maybe you want to simply earn twice as much money as you are making now. Maybe you want to earn ten times more money than you make now. This book will get you on whatever path you are looking to get on. The choice is totally up to you. You can read this book and put it on the shelf to gather dust, or you can read this book and begin the changes that your life deserves. Now, on with the good stuff!

One of my favorite proverbs in the good book comes from Ecclesiastes. The writer says in Chapter 3 "There is an appointed time for everything. And there is a time for every event under heaven … a time to tear down, and a time to build up. A time to weep, and a time to laugh; A time to mourn, and a time to dance."

The writer is trying to say that no matter what is going on in your life, whether it is a great time or the worst time of your life, every moment can be used for good, for the betterment of yourself and for those around you. Coming from a fatherless home and eventually being raised by my aunt and uncle, I was fortunate to learn this concept at an early age. As I grow older, I now see the fruits of what can happen when you have this mindset as you make choices in your life. Life is not to be wasted. It is precious. Sure, we need to enjoy life and have some fun, but there is a huge difference between enjoying life and wasting your life. What if you worked a little bit harder during a time in your life, so that you could enjoy your life even more later? That is what the beginning of this book is about.

Throughout my life these seasons have come and gone, but it wasn't until I was on my own, completely independent, that I learned how this would relate to my career. I was a sophomore in college, and I was about to not only enter into a season of mourning in my life with the loss of my mother, but I was also about to enter into a season of survival. The truth is, as I look back at all the stormy and sunny seasons I've experienced in my life, I already understood that these seasons were here to strengthen me. Little did I know they would form me like clay into the man I am today and into the man I am becoming. These seasons allowed me to have the strength that I would need to endure the next 3 years as the most important part of my life was approaching me -- and I didn't even know it.

In the fall of my junior year I met my future wife Emily. I was a college kid, athlete, and part-time worker at McDonald's, my first job. Somehow I was surviving despite of 20 weekly hours of work, playing baseball, doing well in school and dating this girl. As my feelings deepened for my girlfriend and with finances coming to a crash, it was time. I was 20 years old and I was about to enter into a new season that would change my life. This is the season that each and every one of you needs to enter into if you want to get ahead in life, double your income, and change your lifestyle. I call this season the season of humility and perseverance.

This is the season that will change your life. I had a reason to enter this season. It was because I needed to get ahead in life and marry the woman of my dreams. The aspect of this season we are going to focus on is humility -- not an easy one for all of us to swallow, but an awfully important one. In this aspect, the humility comes in the form of asking for help. If you want to start your journey to changing your lifestyle and goals, you must be willing to ask for help and be persistent.

This season will help you gain experience in the art of selling. You have to sell people on why they should help you. Whether that comes in the form of asking people to help you with your housing situation or asking someone younger and more successful than you about their secrets, you must have humility to be able to complete this season in your life efficiently. You may need to ask your boss for more hours because you're not meeting ends meet. Maybe you need to rent a room out in your home to collect some extra money. Maybe you need to crash on friends' couches (like I did for a little while; I felt homeless). No matter what it is, it will often take humility to realize you aren't there and you need more help in order for you to get there. I entered this season on the sad day that I told my coach that I had to stop playing ball because I needed to support myself. That was humiliating, but I am glad that I made the decision.

WARNING: Do not use this season in your life as a way to become lazy and live off other people, that is not what I am saying, and that is the danger you must be aware of when being "humble."

Perseverance. This is the meat of this season. This is where all the protein and good flavors come from that will give you a reason to live out this season in your life. You must have perseverance to go through this time in your life when everything is telling you not to continue on. You must have the perseverance to dedicate your time, energy, efforts, and mind to changing your life. Sometimes this means working 100 hours a week.

As I entered into this season, everything began to ramp up for me, out of nowhere I was working four jobs, attending school full time (15 credits), and having a relationship with my future wife. I worked at McDonald's, I worked at a retail store, I worked as a plow man during snowstorms, I was a Resident Advisor while I was a full time student, and I was a soon to be engaged, all at the same time. This season lasted for about two years of my life. I worked an average of 70 hours a week, multiple times peaking at 100 hours of work, once during a week in which I completed three final tests in college. I made the dean's list four semesters through this season and earned a Bachelor's Degree. Why did I do this? Because I saw my future. I know what I wanted, so I needed to make this happen. I had to persevere. I wanted to give my incredible fiancé the best wedding, the best home, and the best life possible. The results of living this season of my life? Let me tell you:

During this season I built some incredible friendships and networks along the way. People had no choice but to see the work ethic I had. Not only was I bringing in the money I needed to support my future wife, but I was building shoulders that could do anything in the workforce, and it was being noticed. Everyone notices you whether you are lazy, average, or hard-working.

This season of life came to a bump when I got laid off for the winter from my landscaping job, four months after I quit McDonald's because I was working so much overtime doing the landscaping that it wasn't worth staying at McD's. But I had to persevere onward; I couldn't sit here and do nothing. I needed six more months of crazy amounts of work so that I could take a new step in life through marriage, so I got a gig pumping gas with a college degree. Talk about humility! I had a Bachelors of Science and I was pumping gas. But this step would end up being one of the best career choices I would make because I would meet a man who would change my life, one of my best friends, mentors and my now business partner: Jimmy.

With Jimmy, I worked as many hours as I possibly could while I job-searched, until I got a management gig at Starbucks. My hard work was starting to pay off! I got hired on as a manager! I worked two jobs for two more months in my life until a new season in my life changed. That season I call the season of taking risk.

The season of risk is that step that you must take after you have settled in comfortably to working 70 hours. Think about what you just read. You are now comfortable working 70 hours a week! At this point you have to start expanding your mind to the new opportunities that are now out there for you with all your new skills you have learned over your 2-3 years of working an insane amount of hours.

For me, the season of risk started right when I got married and started fostering my two incredible nieces. Not long after that, a colleague came up to me and said you would be perfect for this sales gig. I had never worked in sales, never mind insurance. Both were foreign to me. I was married and had kids and was sitting "comfortably" as a manager at Starbucks making $30,000 a year. As I analyzed the proposal I realized one thing. I wanted more than to be a manager. I want to get ahead in life. I was offered a position to make the same base salary I made and potentially a bonus, which was cool with me, I was sold. I started a new gig as an insurance salesman, with no experience. But the risk was what scared me. If I didn't pass my test in one week, I would be out of a job, no income, and a family at home. But I had to. I had to take the risk. So I did. That risk would change the next two years of my life forever.

Three months after accepting this job, I made the "ludicrous" choice to buy a four-unit multi family home with the help and advisement from my good friend Jimmy. With these choices I not only doubled my income but tripled it in two years. One of my favorite stories as an entrepreneur is the parable of the talents in the book of Matthew, Chapter 25. A talent (an ancient monetary denomination) was worth about 20 years of labor. The owner of the field gave to one worker 5 talents, another worker 2 talents, and another 1. Each man was responsible for doing as he wished with his talents. The man with 5 talents went out and doubled his 5 to 10, the man with 2 doubled his to 4, but the man with 1, simply let his money sit for him, and it didn't nothing for him. This story is awesome because it kind of encourages people to invest, and that people get what they work for.

Let's sum up the action that you must take in order to get onto the path way of 2X more income:

a. Enter into the season of humility and perseverance -- Are you working comfortably at 40 hours a week or less? Do you need to start getting the help you need to gain more income? Now is the time to start this season, the older you get the less you want to do it!

b. Then enter the season of risk -- after you gain the skills and networks that you need to get that job, start that company, or buy that investment that can help you make the income you need to crush life, then go and take the risk. If you plan properly and use the

advice later given in this book, your
risk will not seem like a risk at all!

What season are you in at this time in your life?

_____

_____

_____

_____

**How can you prepare yourself to enter your next
season in life?**

_____

_____

_____

_____

**How are you going to enter into these seasons of
life, what action are you going to take?**

_____

_____

_____

_____

Get Your Money Right

This action almost feels like it should be the easiest one to do, but for some reason I see people having an immense amount of trouble grasping it. That, or they are all talk, no action. Getting your money right has to do with so many different avenues, but there are three main ones I highlight in this chapter. Cut unnecessary spending and bad bills, work your tail off, and relocate your money.

Maybe you are in the middle of the first season discussed in the previous chapter, but you hardly have any money to put away into your savings. You're working 70 hours a week, and saving no money. Maybe you refuse to enter that first season because of obligations you feel that are more important. Or maybe you haven't entered the season of risk! Let's break down these three avenues that can help get your money RIGHT!

We all work hard for every dollar that we earn. Imagine this. You have a stack of 2,000 one-dollar bills. You are driving a constant 60 mph down the street for a few miles. You open the window of your vehicle, and money slowly blows out of the car. By the time you arrive at your destination you have $47 left and you are confused as to what happened to the other $1,953. People do this everyday. To be honest, this is one of the biggest problems I see people do every day!!! Worst of all I see people do this and not even care!

People are afraid to talk about their finances and have the humility to have someone help them with it. Listen, stop being caught up in having to have the latest car, expensive cable, high-priced insurance, the best of this and the best of that. If you are in the first season of being humble and persevering, then after you get another job and start working more, look at where you are wasting your money! Here are just a few areas where you can re-evaluate to see where you could save money, in order for you to have more financial freedom (to the point where you can start paying for these bills AND save money to invest, wouldn't that be nice!):

    a.   Car payments – Avoid the lease, if you can barely afford your bills. If you're not in a financial position to lease, then don't do it. Are you paying an unnecessary car note of $400 while having bigger obligations to attend to like providing a home for your family or investing for retirement? Then I recommend you downgrade or drive a beater for a few years. Spending money on a vehicle is one of the worst financial decisions you can make if you are struggling financially, so until you get there either don't do it, or do it small.

b. Cable, Phone, and Internet Service – the first question, do you need cable? If not, stop it altogether. Very simple. If you plan on getting your money right, you shouldn't even have time to watch TV. in the first place! If you need it and the competitor can offer the same package for $50 a month less, switch. Either that or call your cable company and ask them to lower your bill; they usually will. Have a nice phone for one main reason -- business. Don't use it to mainly to play games, use it to make thousands of dollars.

c. Insurance – Are you paying a $400 car note and $300 on insurance, and have $0 in your savings or retirement account? Make sure you shop. Stop wasting money on a car, shop the insurance (it's free to shop and if you can save $20 a month, switch), and lower those bills to $300 a month.

Next, work your tail off. Listen, the point is if you don't have what you need you must go get it. Become a go getter, so you can become a giver. Increase your income by dedicating more time to work! This is a season we all need to have multiple times in our life! If you aren't doing this at all you are wasting your life more likely than not. This step mixed with the previous step can become a lethal weapon in your goal to doubling your income. Imagine you save yourself $300 a month and you increase your income $800, you now are making an extra $1,200 a month, also known as $14,000 extra back into your pocket! Common sense, guys, seriously. That is what I am talking about!

The last and perhaps the MOST important part of the three steps to getting your money right is the relocating of your money. Now that you have $14,000 extra a year, what should you do with it? You certainly shouldn't go buy brand-new car or big-screen TV. I mean, that's pretty obvious by now. Here is my recommendation. This is the recommendation that is changing my life as you read this. Save that money, to invest that money. This is a key to doubling your income.

I found my success in real estate investment. My one four- unit was able to offer me an additional $25,000 a year, AND I lived in one of the apartments. Talk about one of the best choices I ever made with getting my money right! For many getting to this point alone could help you double your income in two years! Wouldn't that be nice! With this math you have $14,000 from savings and working, more plus the $25,000 from your investment, you now make $39,000 extra in cash, dinero, paper per year!

Listen as you go through the two major seasons we discussed in chapter one, take these three areas of your life and re-evaluate your financial condition.

a. Control your finances, don't be afraid to save money
b. Work more hours, bring more income in (ethically and legally!).
c. Relocate your money so your money, works for you, you don't just work for money!

BUDGET AND GET YOUR MONEY RIGHT!

Payment	Currently paying	Could Pay
Monthly Car Payment		
Car/Home Insurance		
Heat/Electric Utilities		
Cable and Internet		
Phone		
Rent and Mortgage		
Food and Beverage		
Recreational Spending		

Get Uncomfortable

Many people live life trying to be as comfortable as possible, making sure they take on as little risk as possible. They were told from a young age to get an education, work 40 hours a week, and settle down so hopefully you can retire when you are between ages 60 or 70. We have been taught that this is a comfortable life. Then you reach 70 years old, you barely have enough in your bank account to live for the next five years, Social Security is gone and you may have 30 more years to live. I know every single one of us has experienced the difficulty of seeing someone not have enough for retirement and struggle the rest of his or her life. That's because they decided they just wanted to live a simple comfortable life or they weren't educated enough to change their mindset.

As you live a comfortable life, you may start to realize as you read this book that you haven't truly been comfortable at all. That is good, because it is the beginning of getting into the good uncomfortable life that you should be living! Good uncomfortable life? You are always losing me, Josh! What do you mean? Thanks for asking! Let me show you three ways of what it takes to get uncomfortable, and what it truly means!

Humility. Ruh oh, as Scooby would say. That tough word has come back to haunt us! Humility,

humility humility, dig it in your brain, and not just the way you were taught as a kid growing up (because you need to have confidence in your life), but in a new sense. Have the humility to say to yourself "I don't have it all together; in a matter of days or months my life could collapse, I need to do more than what I am doing." Build a new urgency in your life! Once you do this to yourself, you will be able to start being uncomfortable.

Being uncomfortable is the only way to truly gain the comfort and freedom you are looking for in life. When you go to the gym, you strain your muscles, your lungs, and your body. You begin to feel extremely uncomfortable. But for some reason you keep going and you keep doing it to yourself. We all know why. It's because you have wired your brain to realize that exhausting yourself now will help you be stronger and be less prone to disease later, you become uncomfortable now, so you can be comfortable later.

The same goes with your finances, income, and goals for retirement. We have to humble ourselves and realize that everything we were taught as a kid may not be correct when it comes to success, finances, and goals. If you flex your financial muscles, work them out, work yourself out to earn more income, control your finances and make choices that you haven't been taught to make, you will set yourself up for financial comfortability in your future. It starts with being uncomfortable right now.

As I said earlier, for two years I worked 70 hours a week, while a college student, and dating the love of my life. I can promise you one thing. My body and mind were uncomfortable. I could barely keep my eyes open most days. I got very sick twice, when I had not been sick in eight years. My brain was always exhausted, yet somehow I still pumped out good grades. As I look back on these days in my life, I consider them to be the key foundational parts in my life that taught me what it takes to create a financial future for myself. Getting uncomfortable was the best decision I ever made for my career.

How can you become uncomfortable today? Obviously it starts with stepping away from all the relaxing, asking people for help, and putting your body and mind to work. Now, I am about to give you some easy golden nuggets that you have had sitting right in front of you all along.

a. *Get a second job* – Maybe you have a pretty good job now, or a job you like, but you're working 40 hours or less per week. Well guess what, you're too comfortable. Go get a second job, work 60-plus hours a week. Start a business that can create profitable income for yourself. Go do something to increase your net worth and build your savings, because once you do, you can get to a point where you can invest!

b. *Go get a different job* (and then either cut the hours at your current job, or if you leave, go back to step A and get a second job!). Maybe you are the person who has had the same job for 20 years, making barely enough money, always living paycheck to paycheck. Maybe you just aren't in a field where you can make a ton of dough. Then, maybe it's time to re-evaluate your job title. Maybe you should go into sales, which is one of the best jobs in the world that can help you create income! Why? Because you are always selling! You are either selling yourself to someone, or selling yourself to yourself, that you just can't do it. Change your mindset! Go get the money that is yours for the keeping!

c. *Network* – We have all heard the cliché "it's all about who you know." Well listen, it's true! Go out there and spread your wings! If you're shy, get uncomfortable, say hello to strangers. The more you work, the more jobs you have, the more people you will know. If you are a hard worker, you prove yourself, you will find the right people to surround yourself with, the right clientele that you can sell to, and your boss may now be a friend and business partner because he saw the truth about you through your work ethic! The more people you know, the more likely you will make more money, so network! Your network is your net worth!

d. *Drain (train) yourself* – Stop working a measly 40 hours a week. That is nothing! Go out there and get the income you need to build a future for yourself! Look for options to make more money, get more work, get a better job, or start a business. There would be no need for a website like www.indeed.com, if there wasn't work available out there! Go work more!

e. *Invest in yourself* – Do you want to make more money? Well, there is only one way that spending money on yourself can help you make more money. That is through investing in your education, training, and mentorship. You need to stop being comfortable with wasting thousands of dollars on a depreciating asset, and begin relocating your money into yourself. Train your skills like selling through Grant Cardone. Were you able to spend thousands of dollars at college? Do you waste thousands of dollars on depreciating assets? Well it's time for you to start spending hundreds and thousands toward training yourself to become better at something that can help you make money! I have a list of recommendations, including Cardone University, Keys to Success for Kids, etc…if you start investing in your sales techniques and training your mindset, I promise you will start making more money! Need a mentor? Contact me! www.joshtherrien.com

    Listen, I have given you loads of information so far on how you can start doubling your money and truly creating financial wealth and freedom for yourself. Those ways have all been tested, tried, and true. I have done all of this, and it works! As you go through the different seasons in your life and as you get your money right, you can then start the ultimate test of getting uncomfortable and training your body, mind, and spirit to making more income for your home. It is your duty and obligation. You owe it to your family to create a better financial future for all of you!

To purchase product from Cardone Enterprises simply visit:

http://www.grantcardone.com/?ref=MakeAChangeInc

All purchases donate 20% towards Make-A-Change Inc.

List Your Goals: Where Are You and Where Do You Want to Go?

_____

_____

_____

_____

_____

_____

_____

_____

_____

_____

_____

_____

_____

_____

_____

_____

_____

_____

_____

_____

_____

_____

_____

_____

_____

_____

_____

_____

_____

_____

Now and Later

Now and later … now, that was a classic candy. But let's be honest for a minute about anyone who has had this candy. Whoever waited later to eat them? Who saved them for later if they started eating one? I would eat the whole package when I got some! Why? Because waiting later was a terrible idea. Let me tell you, when it comes to your financial life, it's a terrible idea to wait to get your money right!

After I got married and started working in insurance sales I said to myself, I am sick of renting, I want to own my home NOW! I couldn't wait, I wanted it now. I felt like I was throwing money out the window every time I sent a rent check out. Do not stop paying your rent, but explore other opportunities, maybe opportunities that can create income for yourself like I did.

As I was house shopping, I wanted at least a 3 or 4 unit. It simply made sense; I could live in it and have 2 or 3 other people help pay the expenses of the home. This would bring in at least another $1,000 a month that I would normally be sending out for rent. We looked at what felt like 100 homes! There were four properties that we found particularly a good deal for our family and we knew they were the home we should buy. Being first-time home buyers, we decided to take a day or two after looking at each house to make sure this was what we wanted to do. In those couple days we would end up losing every house to another offer that had been submitted before us. We were waiting too long. We were almost out of options in our town that we wanted to buy and live in.

Then one evening we went to a home that just went on the market with in the last five days. It was a 4-unit building that needed some work, but would easily pay for the bills and put $1,500 a month back into my pocket. I remember standing in the street looking at my realtor and saying, "Listen, after losing four homes that we wanted because we waited too long, we have had enough. We want to put the offer on this house NOW! If we wait a day we could lose this house, too!"

Boy did we make the right choice in deciding to change our financial future at that moment instead of waiting! The next two months went on and finally we closed on October 1, 2014. The decision to make the offer NOW at that very point in time, is why we were able to obtain the best investment I could have ever made at that time in my life.

Many people don't realize how fragile their financial future truly is until it's too late. That is why I am writing this book. I am creating ideas to provoke thought in your head about different ways that you could be thinking about money that you aren't. Have you ever looked at http://www.usdebtclock.org/ ? It's scary. If you think Social Security is going to be around forever, I hate to inform you but, that is very unlikely. What if the economy crashed today? Would you be ready to withstand it? Do you realize that the average wage raise in the workforce is lower than the inflation rate? Wouldn't you like to have more control of your future, finances, and assets? Then take heed to the stories in this book, it can help you if not a lot, at least a little.

If you look back on many of the stories in this book you realize a constant theme:. *Now. Now. Now.* I needed to get married now, because I loved her. I had to switch my job now, because I could make more money. I had to produce more sales now, because I needed to duplicate my income. I needed to buy my house now, I was sick of wasting my money. Here is a list of **nows** that you should embrace:

- Stop wasting your money, now
- Start earning more money, now
- Change your mindset, now
- Invest in your skills, now
- Save to invest, now
- Invest, now
- Get uncomfortable, now
- Read this book and take action, now
- You get it? NOW!

Enough about now, Joshua. Tell me about later! Listen I have harped on NOW in this chapter because it is the essential part to your life and the part that gives oxygen and life to your later! Are you someone who wants to enjoy a nice vacation? Have time with your kids? Pay for your kids' college? Have the ability to pay any medical bill at any time? Do you want to have the chance to help unfortunate people across the world? Well, getting your NOW fixed, will set up your later for a beautiful success. Instead of relying on the government or on fluctuating stocks, rely on your own assets through your own gifts and real estate. Once you do this, other doors will open for you!

I remember being told that I shouldn't get married young, it was a bad decision, wait and do it later. Looking back at it I wouldn't have been able to travel the world like I have with my best friend, my wife! I also wouldn't have been able to travel the world like I have if I hadn't gotten my money right. Not only am I able to enjoy the now because of the groundwork and foundation I have built for my family, but now I can assure more and more every day with every investment in myself and in my assets, that I can enjoy later, too.

You only live once, YOLO. I love this statement. Not because it gives me the license to go and drink, smoke, and mess around as much as I like. What it does to me is give me the drive, motivation, and ability to live my life to its ABSOLUTE fullest, that way as I grow older in life I can enjoy what I have been given due to my hard work, persistence, and choices. I only live once. So I want to truly live life to my full potential. Each and every one of you has a human body, that is fully capable of being amazing, and you have to live in the now so you later can truly exemplify the YOLO way of life!

It's like this. Each and every one of these steps can build on the other. They can be used together and help make a better financial future for you and those who are surrounded by you. Here is the cycle that you need to put in your life now to ensure an incredible later. Create more income where you work by working more, get another job and network, which we will discuss later in this book.

Getting a second job that can build off your main job would be ideal. Then, save as much money as you possibly can. When you start to earn more money do not go and create a better lifestyle for yourself! Live low for a little and save your extra earned money. Why save? You save to invest. Investing will be the most incredible part of your money earning paths. Waiting and saving up a ton of money for the RIGHT investment will create a financial vehicle you will be happy you created. When the time is right for you to invest, do your research, talk to people who have been there, and be mentored by someone successful in the investing world. I guarantee you will be making a ton more money than you imagined if you follow everything in this book.

Where are you now in your life?

_____

_____

_____

_____

_____

How can you change your life now?

_____

_____

_____

_____

_____

Where do you see your self in two years?

_____

_____

_____

_____

_____

Motivation and Networking

There are two major aspects of motivation. Motivation is both self-created and it is received by those with whom you are surrounding yourself. Two classic statements come to mind as I think about motivation. The first we have all heard is "The early bird gets the worm" and the second is "Bad company corrupts good morals."

The early bird gets the worm. Let's take a moment to really think about what this means. The earlier the bird gets going on its journey for the day, the more likely it will be successful in getting its life to be fully fulfilled throughout the day by catching the best and juiciest worm for itself and its offspring. The same goes with you. This can be both applied to the chapter we just read, while being implemented into your every-day plans. By getting your financial life on the right pathway now, you can enjoy your valuable life later. The part I want to focus on now about being the early bird, however, has to do with your everyday habits and schedule.

Are you someone who needs to sleep 10 hours a day? Do you work late-night shifts, so it allows you to sleep until 9 or 10 a.m.? I think you know the point I am going to go with this. It's time to stop wasting your time and get the most out of every hour of everyday. For me, personally, I go to bed at 11:30 p.m. most nights and I wake up at 6:30 a.m. most days. Truthfully, my goal is to wake up at 5:30 a.m., because seriously, 24 hours in a day just is not enough. Throughout my day I try to read a minimum of 30 pages a day, pray, work a minimum of two income producing jobs or projects, educate myself, spend time with my wife and kids, and go to the gym.

I have trained myself and created habits in my body where I can now do more throughout my day and feel great all day. I work six days a week, and spend time with my family and my faith on the seventh. Oh, and on the seventh day I still do something that can help me expand my income, education, and network. Every day is a day that we can use to live life in every shape and form. To this day, I am working on figuring out how I can do more in my day, and minimize distractions.

The persons who commits themselves to their financial future will have a financial future. Your financial future is affected by every hour of every day, by realizing this, you will make more money. You need to wake up every single day and motivate yourself. Without the ability to motivate yourself it will make it harder to complete this part of your life.

Bad company corrupts good morals. The main point of this statement has to do with your morals in life. If you surround yourself with drugs, thieves, temptations, and negative people, I guarantee, you will become just like those you have surrounded yourself with. A hard part of deciding to surround yourself with the right people will be the friends that you may not want to be around anymore. But listen -- if a friend isn't helping you progress in life, are they really a friend? I do not advocate this meaning to leave a spouse; that is one area where I encourage working out your life and grow together.

The part of your life that must be changed by this philosophy is your sphere of influence. The people you're surrounding yourself with, will not just affect your morals but also your financial status in life. By being around people who will motivate you, it will make motivating yourself much easier to accomplish. Surrounding yourself with people who work hard daily, have similar goals to you, will make attaining your goals much better.

Being with people who have been successful and are better than you, is one of the biggest keys to getting to where you want to be. Grasping the understanding that there are people who are better than you and who have done what you are trying to do, is also one of the most important humbling steps to gaining more financial, spiritual and physical aptitude. I'm not saying better as in their souls are more important, but in the sense that they are where you want to be, so they set the bar and standard for what you as a person want to strive to be like.

Networking can help you create this impact that you are trying to impose on yourself. There was a story that I heard -- I forget the source -- where an entrepreneurial business owner opened a restaurant in order to help create a network for his business and work to create a bigger customer base and make money at the same time. You see, there are three ways that each of us who want to create more income must network: (1) to create more customers (leads, etc.); (2) to create great business relationships (promotions, business start-ups, etc.); (3) and to build tight-nit relationships for your power squad, which is your main guys whom you go to war with on your road to a more financially free future. One of those networking techniques is guaranteed to help you in one way or another, let's break them down:

All three networking opportunities can help you do one thing: create more income in your life. Creating a bigger customer base starts with figuring out who has your money and reaching out to them in order to create a bigger commission for yourself in one way or another. Maybe this will be through your first or second job, but one huge golden nugget for your two or more jobs is to make sure that they can directly affect each other in a positive way so that you can expand your wallets together.

For example, a great second job for a car salesman maybe to sell auto insurance on the side, and therefore, every car that they sell can also lead to the sale of insurance. As a result, every insurance customer that they have will know that he also sells cars for when they decide to go shopping. The two jobs directly relate to each other and cannot only increase that person's income, but can increase the income from both jobs.

There are many different ways to expand your professional and business network. One obviously good way is through LinkedIn, an online professional networking website. Other ways can be through the job at which you work by building great relationships within the organization and with those who are in management, thus opening the door for potential promotions … which does what? It can help expand your income. Other ways are by traveling to different events to meet people you don't know!

Maybe the one person that you created a great relationship with someday goes elsewhere and remembers you specifically for the relationship you built with him, and thinks you're the person for a new job opening elsewhere with better pay. Or maybe you start your own business someday through your investments and the network you built and created planted seeds that can help grow you and your company. You will hear every successful business person all say two things: *Network and be mentored*. Mentorship will be covered in a later chapter.

Last, networking for your power squad. Grant Cardone calls this your power base. These will be the people you hand-in-hand grow with and help through friendships, referrals, and just one great mutual relationship. These will be the main people who will encourage you to push harder and do better. Your relationship will result in great tangible benefits for one another, like referrals. We said earlier, who is truly a friend? It is those who encourage you to do better, push harder, and are there for you when you go through not only the ups, but also the downs.

How can you expand your network today?

_____

_____

_____

_____

List your power squad and why they are
important

_____

_____

_____

_____

How are you held accountable to push hard 24/7?

_____

_____

_____

_____

Choices

Isn't that a broad chapter title? Choices. Merriam-Webster's dictionary defines a choice as "the opportunity or power to choose between two or more possibilities: the opportunity or power to make a decision." The choice is one of the most powerful weapons in the world. It is the very thing that determines your future. Choices can either destroy you or build you up. We all have to understand one thing though. Every single thing we do, every action we take, it is totally and 100 percent your very own, choice.

Unfortunately, making excuses is one of the greatest choices to many people, and it is either the greatest downfall to many or it creates the perfect road to being average and comfortable. We hear it all the time from problems like drugs to simple problems like time. Too often we hear "poor me, poor me," yet there is no action from that person. They are stagnating with no point for growth. They believed the lie that we were all taught growing up, instead of expanding their mind to figuring out what is truly out there.

Three of the greatest excuses I want to go over will be some of the most common that I hear and I believe are some of the biggest problems people face today. Each one of these can be controlled by your choices and changed for the better: Time, lack of inheritance, and complaining without doing anything.

Time. Boy does this one make me cringe. We all hear people say all the time, "I have no time for this or that … blah, blah, blah." I mean, honestly, this one curdles my stomach! I know people who work 60 hours a week, have five meetings a day, sell 10 products, answer 500 texts and 15 calls a day, yet somehow it is they who are not the ones complaining; oh, and they read a book in between it all. It's the individual who works 40 hours a week, has two days off, sometimes three with a holiday, and they say there is not enough time in the day, yet they have 128 more hours in their week to accomplish a whole lot more!

If you read this book, and you are beginning to follow the lessons in this book, I guarantee your financial life and overall lifestyle will become better. As a result, I want you all to embed one thing in your head: there is enough time, there is always enough time, for what you prioritize. Don't use your kids, your wife, your occupation, or anything as an excuse for not having enough time. We are all busy, so being busy isn't an excuse for anyone. To put it in perspective, I read 1 book a week, work seven days a week, watch a few educational videos, spend time with my kids and wife … oh, and I still have enough time to get more done. If there is ever a down time in my life, I make sure I fill it with something productive, I never use time as an excuse, and neither should you.

Lack of inheritance. Oh boy. This is a fun one. "But Josh, I wasn't blessed to inherit a bunch of money to become financially free, and Tim over there, well he was given everything by his uncle Donnie." Whenever I hear something like that it sounds a lot like the teacher from Charlie Brown speaking, "Wah, wah, wuh, wah, wah, wah." Yeah, it's crap. Your family heritage has no connotation on the choices you make for your family be set free. It's your turn to step up and make a name for your family!

I had no father by the time I was 1 year old, lost my mother by the time I was 19, both to drug addiction, I had $40 to my name at 20, and guess what, I still came out every day with a goal to change my life and my family name, and one day, people will remember the Therrien name for the good that was brought to this world because of the choices that I decided to make in my life! You can do it, too. Set your goals today so you don't have to continue making excuses like this, because guess what? In two years if you made an extra $10k a year, and saved every dime, you would have $20k in the bank, enough to make some sort of investment to contribute to doubling your income!

Complaining without doing anything. The third biggest mistake people make when creating excuses about their situation is complaining and then doing nothing about it. To be frank, everyone has his own problems and realizes that it's all our own choice to be where we are to a certain extent. Now, sure, there are some things that we can't control, like health problems and whatnot, but if you had read and taken to heart anything in this book, there are still ways to doubling your income and creating a financial freedom that you and your family deserve, if you decide to make the choice to put the effort into changing your status in life!

I guarantee that if you change your choices and make a change in your life, things can get better for you as long as they are the right choices. These are choices that align with the teachings and recommendations of those who have gone through it before.

The choices we make build off everything that we have gone over since the beginning of this book. It takes a choice to enter into a season of hard work and a choice to decide to take the step to double your income. It takes a choice to spend your money wisely and save it properly in order to help find financial freedom for yourself. It takes choices to work harder at your job to gain a pay raise or work a second job.

Choices are what will change your financial path, I guarantee it.

Today's choices are a direct result of where you will be tomorrow. If you want to double your income, make the proper steps towards doing that very thing! No one is going to give it to you with the snap of two fingers. What are you going to do after reading this? Are you going to complain that you don't have enough time in your day, or are you going to create and buy time? Are you going to blame others for your circumstances, or make strides to change your own life? Are you going to sit down and continue to watch TV, play video games, and stay in the same lifestyle you have lived in for the past years, or are you going to finish this book and start making choices to better your life?

Create a general schedule for yourself

Time	
12:00 am	
1:00 am	
2:00 am	
3:00 am	
4:00 am	
5:00 am	
6:00 am	
7:00 am	
8:00 am	
9:00 am	
10:00 am	
11:00 am	
12:00 pm	
1:00 pm	
2:00 pm	
3:00 pm	
4:00 pm	
5:00 pm	
6:00 pm	
7:00 pm	
8:00 pm	
9:00 pm	
10:00 pm	
11:00 pm	

Advice and Mentors

This is one of my favorite chapters in this book and I am only saying that based upon the title I gave this chapter having no idea what my fingers are going to type over the next few hours. I have had so many sources of advice in my life, much of which I am very grateful for because it has helped mold me into the man I am today and who I will be tomorrow. The great thing about this chapter is it builds upon the very thing you should be doing as you read this book: gaining advice and mentorship. By the end of this book I want to be among your many mentors, and I am going to give a one-time offer at the end of this chapter!

We have already gone over how important it is to surround yourself with the right people. This information we are about to go over builds off that premise. Let me start off by giving some advice we have all heard probably once in our lives.

I'm going to go on a whim here, honestly, and say that most people in life have been advised at least once by someone that they must go to college and complete a degree. Although I did this myself, and it did help expand my mind and train me in the long run of education, I tell you it was not the only choice I had. At the time I didn't know that, though. I truly feel like much of college was a waste, but that does not mean I don't think many people should pass it up. The truth is, though, there are many ways to climbing the corporate ladder and gaining incredible financial success without a degree. The same does not go for knowledge and education, though. Truth is, the best way to double your income is by educating yourself. It does not require a college degree; all it requires is determination and focus on proper education. There are plenty of licenses like insurance sales, real estate sales, mortgage sales, and many others that require one thing to begin with: a license. A license that you are educated on that subject and continue to educate yourself on long after you have received it. Education is a life-long experience; it should never stop, but it should be the proper education. No one has ever taught you how to sell, how to budget, how to double your income, yet these are some of the most important things for your career!

I have received a lot of advice in my life. Let me start with a few incredible pieces of advice that truthfully, was the worst thing someone could have told me. Just before I go into these advices I was told, let me start off with the key to receiving advice. If you are going to listen to what others say, you must ask the following question: "Was this person successful at what they are advising me about?" If you answer "no" to this questions, there is a very,

very high chance you should not be listening to this advice.

I'll never forget when I got engaged to my beautiful wife. She was only 18 years old, a senior in high school, and I was a ripe 21 finishing up college. I can't even count the number of times that I was told the worst advice I could receive about marrying my future wife. It seemed like everyone and their Aunt Sue was an expert about marriage. I was told not to get married but to enjoy my life, I was told that I wasn't financially set to get married, I was told that I should live with her a little before I married her. The decision to help foster two of my beautiful nieces right before marriage? Oh, forget it, I was a lunatic. One consistent pattern I realized with everyone who gave me this advice was that they all failed at least once at marriage or they had absolutely no experience with marriage! They were destroying an incredible sacred act because of the bad choices of many before or around them!

As I was deciding which home to buy when I bought my first multi-family home, I found the strangest thing happening. Once again, everyone was all of a sudden an expert in renting out multi-families and purchasing property! Maybe renting out homes isn't for everyone, I get that, but truth is everyone who was advising me this and that had one thing in common. No experience in managing a multi-family, or one bad experience to renting out their single family home. They just didn't have any success at it, so they thought it be best to advise me against the very thing that would someday help create incredible financial wealth for me someday.

The last and one of the best choices I ever made was to go into a partnership. Now this isn't a book about partnerships or what advice I would give about those different life choices, that would be saved for a mentorship lesson, but I tell you what partnerships are an extremely valuable tool to have when starting and running a business. You have to have the right team, the right integrity, and the perfect ingredients for a good partnership to succeed, but if you have never had a partnership or started a business, you should not be giving advice, and you should not be listening to people who haven't done one either!

The best businesses and entrepreneurs have one thing in common; they take advice from the people who have been there before, and have been successful at the very thing they are looking to do. You want to own an apartment complex? Take advice from those who have been great at it! Want to start a business? Listen to people who have done it before! I guarantee, it will make things a whole lot easier for you when making the right decision.

Something that I am extremely grateful for are the mentors who I have had and been able to watch over the last several years. Personally, my goal has been not to just double my income but to really increase my income tenfold. As I listen to people whom I now consider my mentors, teaching me over the years, they all said one thing in common, have a mentor -- someone who can push you to the next level, who you can watch from afar and learn from.

I have also been taught to not be afraid to invest in such mentorships, whether it be in the form of training or meetings, because these investments help shape your mind and your wallet. Investing a few hundred here or a couple thousand there could be the difference between you and tens of thousands of dollars. So I have truly had to figure out who the people are who I should listen to, read books from, and purchase training and webinars from in order to help me get on the financial path I want to get on. Now, there aren't just financial and career mentors, there are spiritual mentors, physical mentors, life mentors, family mentors, and many other kinds of mentors. Here is a list of who my mentors are and why:

Spiritual

1. My parents – they changed my life, they truly showed me what faith was, how to live it, and why I should live it. My aunt and uncle are two of the most incredible saints I know, if you want to know more about them trust me, I would be happy to talk about them.
2. Voddie Baucham – this man has such a passion for righteousness and such a raw

honest love for people, he is a man I sure want to emulate in my home.

I could name many more incredible pastors and people who are an inspiration to my growth in my faith.

Physical

1. Mark Verstegen – having a degree in exercise science, I truly gained a passion for this guy because what he teaches was true functionality in my health, something I truly appreciate.

Family Mentor

1. Again, my aunt and uncle fall in this category, too. They sacrificed for each other, for countless kids, and for me having changed my life.
2. Caleb Maddix and Emily Shai's families - the father-son relationship that Caleb and Matt inspires me to keep growing toward being the man I desire to be. The family bond that I see with Emily's family is beautiful.

Business and Financial Mentor

1. Grant Cardone – this guy has changed my life in my career, his training in sales has taught me that sales isn't just about your job, it is your life! Everything you do is a sale! He has accumulated mass wealth through multiple companies, including real estate!

2. Than Merrill – this guy has had a hit TV show, flipped hundreds of homes, and has started an incredible course called Fortune Builders, which I have had the pleasure of being a student, too.
3. Cole Hater – this guy has also found incredible success through real estate, he is a big family man, who makes sure that throughout all his success and all his downs that he had experienced, he never forgets his why. What's your why? Why do you want to grow? Your why will be a motivator for you in your life.

Other people I listen to when it comes to business advice? Man, the list is long. Gary Vaynerchuck, Robert Kiyoswaki, Warren Buffett, the list is endless.

Who are your mentors? Who are the people in your life that will help you grow throughout the years? If you are looking for a true mentorship I would like to let you know that I would be happy to be your guy. Every year I am going to offer a select number of student's access to my personal mentorship and select scholarships towards completing the mentorship. With the mentorship you will get an 6 hours a year with personal live interaction with me via video call where we can discuss who you are, what your goals are, and how we can help you get there.

It is an investment into yourself, into the motivation that you need to get the most out of life! This mentorship will be one that encourages you to get on the path and mindset to more and more financial freedom. For more information, visit www.joshtherrien.com and send in your request to be mentored today. There are limited spots, so if you want to get on your pathway quicker, prove that you are ready through telling me why you are ready, and then make the investment into your future! Think about what the investment of this book will be bringing you, imagine being able to get live personal interaction for your direct growth! Seriously, get a mentor, I guarantee it will help you in your walk in life!

Who are your mentors?

Spiritual

_____

_____

Physical

_____

_____

Family Mentor

_____

_____

Business/Financial Mentor

_____

_____

Who do you want to be your mentor?

_____

_____

_____

_____

Why do you want them to mentor you?

_____

_____

_____

_____

Illuminate: Your "Why?"

As a young boy I had gone through many hardships, of which I lost my dad and my mother to addiction, while I was a little devil. I was destined to be a statistic. But there were different plans for me. My amazing aunt and uncle raised me to get out of the life I was heading toward. They taught me faith, love, and discipline. Little did they know, they were changing my life, as a direct effect I would grow up to be the man I am today. I tell you this because it has immensely impacted what my why is in life.

You may be wondering what I mean by *What is your why?* Your why is the very thing in your life that helps keep your mind focused. It helps keep your mind driven and determined to complete the goals in your life. They are the deep desires of your heart. It's the change that you want to make in your family, the difference you want to make in this world. It's your fuel that keeps you going every day. We need more people in this world with a why that will change the world.

I learned about the importance of your why through a three-day conference I attended through Fortune Builders. One of the most incredible speakers I have ever listened to, Cole Hatter, helped pull this out of me. I always knew my why deep down, but Cole encouraged me to bring it to the top of my list because if I do so, I will never have a reason to look back and slack.

Cole had some incredible whys in his life. He wanted to become wealthy to help children who were being trafficked, he built orphanages in Mexico, and of course, he gave his wife and his little girl the best life possible. He really hit home for me because it seemed like our stories were so similar. You read this book and you read a lot about money, wealth, and freedom. Let me tell you what really is driving me deep down inside of my heart.

You may have gotten hints here and there about having some tough breaks in life as I grew up as a kid. One day I will write a book about the story of my life to show you what I had to go through to get where I am today. But I want you to understand one thing as you read the rest of this chapter. My upbringing directly affected what my why in life is. Maybe your life wasn't awful, maybe it was worse than mine, regardless, for you to truly keep yourself accountable and motivated you have to figure out what your why is. For your family's sake, find your why, and then create more financial freedom for them!

Everything I am going to be explaining to you stems from one part of my heart. My faith. It is my faith that has helped me determine my why in life, because I experienced what faith can do when going through storms. My biggest reason for being so driven for financial freedom is first to make much of my faith, and then for my entire family. I have seen the pain inside a completely broken person who seemed hopeless and lost their life due to their choices.

Seeing my mother homeless as a little boy, being able to do nothing about it, and then losing her left a scar on my life that will never fade away. I want to give my family freedom from that feeling. My sisters, my aunt and uncle, my nieces, my nephews, my wife, my children, they are all my biggest reason for gaining more financial freedom. I don't want to ever have to say, I can't pay for your medical bills, or I can't give you memories and have amazing times with my family, or I can't help you when you lose your job and potentially lose your home. I am not going to sit back and be that guy. Instead, I am going to be the guy who changes my family for generations.

We have all heard that money can't buy happiness. My whole mind flipped upside down when I realized that is one of the biggest lies that we have been taught our entire lives! There has just been the biggest earthquake an area has ever seen -- devastating lives, people dying, losing limbs, losing their family. And there is nothing you can do about it. You're sad, they're sad, and there is nothing you can do about it. Children are being neglected in broken homes, parents aren't caring about their future as much as their next fix, and there is nothing you can do about it. When you have the ability to fly to another country at the snap of a finger, bring water, food, doctors, home, hope, love, and faith to a devastated area, family, or country, and you see women's smiles, or that little kid's laugh of happiness while starving because you gave him a piece of bread and water, are you going to tell me that you aren't going to be happy that you could do that? Are you going to tell me that having the ability to make an incredible impact in an orphan child's life isn't going to bring happiness not only to yourself but to the children and communities you are helping? I would have to say you may need to rethink that teaching! Money can buy the most incredible happiness when you use it as a tool for whatever good you are called to use it for.

I am driven because of children. There are so many children in this world who don't have the aunt and uncle I had, or the missionary going overseas to bring light into their lives. My goal in life is to have the ability to do this. I want to be able to spend a month in a foreign land to bring love and care to a group of orphan children. The ability to say I am going to fly to Africa in the blink of an eye. Or the ability to help thousands of neglected children in America who are starving for love, hope and guidance.

Children are the most vulnerable people in the world, they can't control their situation much, and so often their lives can be ruined because no one was there to truly love them. I want my family and I to be the difference in these kids' lives! Whether it be bringing kids memories, homes, or simply food, we have to make a difference in their lives.

This is why we started our non-profit Make-A-Change Inc. We are dedicated to helping children going through hardship due to neglect, abuse, or drug addiction. We plan on impacting children in America by building memories that they would otherwise never have and providing faith and financial education. We also plan on building orphanages around the world. Make-A-Change isn't just a non-profit though, it's a movement! Check us out at www.makeachangeinc.org to donate, get involved, or purchase merchandise today!

Drug addiction has a huge stinging connotation to me. My father, mother, countless aunts and uncles lost their lives to this awful darkness. I honestly think I can count on one hand the amount of people left in my family because most people died by the time I was 20. I am driven to make a difference in people who are caught in addiction someday. Honestly, I don't know how yet, but it is a huge disaster that needs to be fixed. Too many people's lives are being lost, homes being broken, and children being crushed because of the weight that addiction has on them.

It saddens me when I see people, children, and communities suffering because of simple things we often take for granted like water, books, food and a non-leaky roof over their heads. My companies and I are determined to help people in these conditions, whether this be in North and South America, Africa, or Asia, we are going to make a difference. Building homes, creating wells, schools, farms, whatever it takes we want to make a small dent into this world and help many in it.

As you can see, I have some pretty hefty driving motivations in my life. My why is clearly defined by truly having a heart to make a difference in my family, children, the homeless and the helpless. My why is clearly defined and taking a step back in life and relaxing a little bit will only do one thing, it will prevent these things from happening. It's our duty and responsibility to truly make a difference, and it can all start with one thing: creating better financial freedoms, vehicles, and income for your household to have the abilities to live out your why in your life.

a. **What is your why, what difference do you want to make in your community?**

_____
_____
_____

b. **How about in your family?**

_____
_____
_____

c. **How are you going to make that difference?**

_____
_____
_____

d. **Are your motivations self-driven or others driven? (hint, hint: take self out of this part of your why, you can have your personal goals separate from your why)**

_____
_____
_____

e. **Are you going to look into** www.makeachangeinc.org **today?**

_____
_____
_____

Listen these are just a few questions to ask yourself as you think deep down about what difference you want to make in the world. I truly encourage you to take the step out of your comfort zone, begin the hard work now, so that in the future you can truly make a difference in the world. You, your family, and thousands of people are depending on you.

www.makeachangeinc.org/getinvolved

Takeaways: Go Do It!

There has been a lot covered in this book, some very difficult concepts to accept and swallow. Yes, I understand, but I guarantee they will change your life and financial future. As you ponder on what has been written in this book I want to go over some major take-homes for you to be reminded of as you plan on taking your next step in this amazing crazy world toward more financial freedom.

First and most important, do not ever neglect your family. Your spouse, your children, and your loved ones are much greater investments that you will make. But remember what we learned earlier. Stop saying there isn't enough time in the day to work more, educate yourself, and be with your family. It all has to do with how you allocate your time.

Equally important, never lose your integrity in your pursuit for more financial freedom. If you lose your integrity you lose everything. You lose your family. You lose your job. You lose your money. You lose yourself. I have dedicated my life to pursuing freedom with the utmost integrity in anything I do. I guarantee all will be well with you if you keep your integrity throughout it all. No matter how much money you make, do not compromise your integrity, and maybe more importantly, no matter how hard it is to make money, never compromise your integrity for more financial wealth. If you do, you lose everything.

Stay goal-focused. If you don't have goal's you don't have something to strive toward. Goals create your *why*. They put a fire in your soul to run the race till you reach them. The most successful people write down their goals every day. You, at least, have to write them down and go over them every day. If you make your goal a higher than doubling your income, I guarantee you will be able to reach it if you follow all the steps and lifestyle it takes to double your finances.

My goals:

a.   Double my income, yearly
b.   Live and lead my family by faith
c.   Create financially-freeing investments
d.   Grow my why, www.makeachangeinc.org
e.   Give my family and children the best possible life
f.   Buy 15 passive income properties in the next 5 years

My goals aren't small by any means, but that's what I want. Do you think by setting these goals I will be more likely to reach them than those who set no goals? I guarantee it. Set goals that double your income, then maybe you can begin to set them for 10 or 20 times larger!

Chapter 1. We went over going through different seasons of life. I implore you now to start a new season, a season of working so hard and so smart that you will create a financial freedom for you and your family. Then and only then will you be able to enjoy the season of your hard work, otherwise you will be working hard until you die. You will be living to die, not living to live. You will either take the risk to live, or the risk to live to die.

Chapter 2. You learned how important it was to stop wasting your money and to start finding the areas in your life where you can save. From there, you go and work more and create a second flow of income to help put that extra couple thousand dollars a month into your pocket. Then with all that saved money, you are going to keep saving, until you can invest it into a financial creating source of income. You have to get your money right!

Chapter 3 saw us getting a little uncomfortable. Are you sitting on the couch watching TV after reading this? I hope not! It's time to start making moves! Get uncomfortable finally so you can live comfortably for years to come! Get your work on, even if it means there is a season of working 80 hours a week, training, and living for something bigger! Your comfort zone is your own worst enemy!

Chapter 4 showed us the value of the now versus the later. Living in the now for the later is the only way to ensure you are preparing yourself for financial doubling. Stop using YOLO as a phrase to encourage you to waste your life, but use it to catapult yourself to the financial stature that you are aiming for! If you don't change your life now, later could be too late.

Chapter 5 showed you the importance of waking up every day motivated to kill it. Without such motivation it is going to make it a lot harder to live for your future now. Being able to wake up motivated to grind everyday will naturally help your network to grow, but getting out in the world to expand your network through conferences, meetings, and social media is a must in order to help find an easier way to grow your network!

Are you ready to start making the right choices? That is what **Chapter 6** was about. Make the choice today to start changing your financial prowess! Your choice today, will have a direct impact on what happens to you and your bank account tomorrow. Maybe you need to make the choice to get uncomfortable, to change your lifestyle, to change who you are getting your advice from. Whatever it is, JUST DO IT! Make the choice to change you and your family's life!

Remember what **Chapter 7** teaches, and find your mentors! Many people believe in the concept that no one is better than anyone. Which, in spiritual sense, is 100 per cent the truth! No one is worth more than the other. But when it comes to self-improvement, you have to find people who are better than you. People who have succeeded where you haven't or where you want to succeed. Find those who are better or more experienced than you. Instead of hating them, decide to emulate them!

In **Chapter 8** we covered the importance of your why. Why do you want to have success or your finances in place? It's a lot deeper than just wanting to have a lot of money or nice things. Your why is your gasoline, your fuel that keeps you going every single day! Dig deep inside you, figure out what your *why* is in life! Without it, it can become extraordinarily difficult to be motivated to wake up every day and be driven to succeed more than you already are. Maybe your why is to help generations in your family, or children around the world, help find a cure for a disease, or to stop human trafficking. Whatever it is, do something about it, and use it as your motivation to keep going, every single day!

Finding the financial freedom you want is never going to come easy. Every person or family has to start somewhere. Today is your day to go out there and make a change in your life. Whether you are 60 or 8, it's never too early and never too late to begin your path to a better you, a better life, and a better family. As Caleb Maddix would say, when deciding to make a change in your life, age is just a number!

Did you enjoy this book and find the principles impactful?

_____

_____

_____

_____

What was your favorite chapter?

_____

_____

_____

_____

Would you consider Josh to be a mentor?

_____

_____

_____

_____

I hope you enjoyed this book immensely! I plan on writing more books in the future. If you could please encourage your friends and family to purchase this book it will help immensely in my personal path to entrepreneurship. Remember this book, and many to come, when birthdays and holidays come around for gifts. Don't forget to visit www.joshtherrien.com and www.makeachangeinc.org to get more involved in the change this world needs!